Ghosts
of Dorset

PETER UNDERWOOD

Bossiney Books

Other ghostly titles from Bossiney Books

Ghostly encounters in the South-West   Peter Underwood
Ghosts around Bodmin Moor   Michael Williams
Ghosts of Cornwall   Peter Underwood
Ghosts of Devon   Peter Underwood
Ghosts of North Devon   Peter Underwood
Ghosts of Somerset   Peter Underwood
Haunted inns of Devon   Robert Hesketh
West country hauntings   Peter Underwood

Author's acknowledgements

The author gratefully acknowledges the interest and help he received in the compilation of this work from, among others, his wife Joyce Elizabeth, Michael and Sonia Williams, Mrs Jean Bowerman, Mrs Peter Brown, Hector D Campbell, Mrs Elsie Clark, Simon Esslemont, Dr Peter Hilton-Rowe, Rodney Legg, Commander George Martelli, Sir Christopher Medlycott, Mrs Mary Noble, Mrs Joan Patch, Tom Perrott, Michael Pinney, John Radcliff, Dr Anne Ross, Miss Ellen Short, Graham Smith, Mrs Dorothy E Warren, Miss Joan Whittington and especially Richard Sheppard who generously put his ghost scrapbook at the author's disposal.

This reprint 2017
This edition first published 2006 by
Bossiney Books Ltd, 33 Queens Drive, Ilkley, LS29 9QW
www.bossineybooks.com
First edition published 1988 by Bossiney Books
ISBN 978-1-899383-88-7
Printed in Great Britain by R Booth Ltd, Penryn, Cornwall

Introduction

Dorset, with its hills and chalk downs, its fertile valleys and stone quarries, is perhaps best known as the Wessex of Thomas Hardy, but with its varied coastline and delightful coves it is also a county full of fascinating ghost stories, strange legends and remarkable features.

Where else would you find anything like the Cerne Abbas Giant, 'Britain's most uninhibited monument'; Chesil Bank, a ten-mile long pebble ridge that is unique; the almost land-locked, beautiful and geologically interesting Lulworth Cove; the picturesque, steep and cobbled Gold Hill at Shaftesbury; Maiden Castle, the largest hill-top camp in Britain; the Dorsetshire cursus, a six-mile long double earth-work, the purpose of which is still unknown?

On the other hand where else would you be likely to find a manor with 22 reported ghosts; a world-famous screaming skull; a ghost that disappeared when it was sat upon; a ghostly white donkey; a phantom coach-and-horses story that was used by Thomas Hardy in *Tess of the D'Urbervilles*; a magnificent house with an everlasting bloodstain; an Iron Age camp that is credited with a prehistoric 'Peeping Tom'; a quiet riverside backwater where the air of an accused murderer's suicide still pervades the atmosphere; an ancient bay where a phantom army walks; or a town with a dozen haunted houses?

The ghosts of Dorset are varied and well-documented. As WE Gladstone once said, psychical research (the scientific study of ghosts and other supernatural phenomena) is 'the most important work which is being done in the world – by far the most important'. It seems to me that the branch of psychical research covering spontaneous phenomena, ghosts and haunted houses is the most important of all. For the experienced researcher there is a wealth of phenomena so overwhelming that, as Sir Alistair Hardy once said to me, 'for scientists or anyone else to ignore shows them to be intellectually dishonest'. A portion of the evidence for just a few of the ghosts in just one small county of England is included in this book.

I have sought to mention briefly the better-known and previously published stories of Dorset ghosts and haunted houses but many of the accounts and information included in this volume have never been previously published anywhere.

Peter Underwood

Ashmore

Here we are in the most remote part of Cranborne Chase, an area which is old and quiet, that has long had the reputation and the history of being a secret place. As Eric Benfield says in his *Dorset* (Robert Hale, 1950): 'Probably there are hidden hoards of stolen wealth still lying there now gripped in the roots of some great tree; and no one would ever find the mouldering bones of the cheated parties and unfaithful mates who bled into the grass there, nor the holed skull of an odd Preventive man.'

There is a story that somewhere here, waiting to be found, is a golden coffin. It is a legend that crops up several times in Dorset but Eric Benfield came across the story enough times to make him believe that there must have been some good reason for it to spread and survive as long as it has and, like him, I have hopes that some day a 'great heavy golden coffin will be levered out of Dorset ground'.

Certainly parts of Cranborne Chase have an unsavoury reputation and a distinctive atmosphere, a feeling that is unlike any I have experienced elsewhere and something that some people have felt to be really frightening.

A former member of the Ghost Club sent in the following account of an All Hallowe'en he spent on Cranborne Chase in the late 1920s and I reproduce it exactly as he left it for the Ghost Club archives:

'On a sunny autumn morning Jude and I started forth on one of our day-long rambles on the Chase. She trotted in front of me, slightly at a slant, tail erect, raising deliberately in turn each delicately padded foot. The joy of life was in her veins, as it was in mine...

'And then Jude began to see things. Her jaunty tail went down close between her shapely, slender legs. Her hackles rose. She whistled shrilly through her nostrils. She crossed to the hedge and cowered against it, her eyes riveted on something I could not see; something that obviously took up all the space in that narrow lane. Something that, judging by the expression of almost mad terror in her eyes, was sweeping past, on and over me, as I stood petrified, gaping at her in despair.

'A cold wind whistled round me. I shivered violently on that burning sun-kissed day. Then she turned and stared behind me, where the thing had passed. Then she fled to me and thrust an ice-cold, quivering, damp nose into my trembling hand.

'We crossed a ditch and passing between two ancient trees wandered along a stony track cut through a dense wood. The day was hot. I carried my coat slung across my arm. The trees smelt damp and old and lichen-grown. The place was like a vapour-bath – and yet I shivered and Jude, leaving her trespassing chase after rabbits, pressed close behind me, her nose touching the back of my leg.

'I hurried along, almost gasping for air, glancing furtively to right and left. Something seemed to be watching me as I stumbled and tripped over the sharp and rough stones that made the way so difficult and tiring… something malignant, sinister, unholy. We reached an open space and stepped out of the dark shadows of the plantation on to the breezy open chase. I drank in deep gaspings of the fragant air and raised my face to feel the warm and comforting rays of the sun upon it. And yet – I was not happy. Jude too was unsettled…

'We were in the vicinity of an ancient camp covering several acres. We stood together, silent, waiting: for what we did not know. Away beyond us stood a clump of massed oaks, the probable site of a praetorium.

'Everything was still and silent. Fearful things were happening within the precincts of that camp; cruelty and lust, despair, and a bloody revenge had each in turn been staged there… Shrieks and yells, cries and groans of dying men burst upon our ears. There was the clang of iron on iron. Loud shouts of fiendish triumph and the moans and death-rattles of the slaughtered.

'The awful clamour ceased as abruptly as it had begun, leaving us cowering and cold with fear. The dog – pressed hard against me – was quaking, her sides heaving with panic. I knelt with my arms around her, loving the warm contact and the loud beating of the faithful heart against my hand.

'The great green expanse about me, sweltering in the vivid autumn sunshine, swayed and grew dark. I think I fainted, sinking down into the heather and the bracken…

'On our way home Jude and I were both a mass of jangling nerves. The sudden autumn dusk fell heavily about us, draping us in its blinding, bewildering folds. In every dusky corner Jude saw a spook. Weird noises sounded round us. Uncanny voices chanted overhead. Shadows we could not account for dogged our scurrying steps. Once, I swear, a black shape glided past our shrinking forms in the guise of a huge black hound. Jude cowered, and once again a protesting nose was pressed against my leg, urging me gently forward.

'How thankful we both were to bang the garden gate behind us on all things ghostly and haunting, and to run swiftly up the short drive to warmth and light and friendly welcoming voices. After dinner I piled round me in silence my much-loved books about the Chase. Page after page I turned in search until I found it… a grisly story of a primitive horde, all those dusty years ago, who made a raid on the villages and scattered hamlets and carried off the women as their captives up to the nearby fort, said to be impregnable.

'All night long the hideous orgy went on, the drinking and the feasting; but as dawn began to break the invaders sank into heavy dreamless slumber, and the women seized their chance. Stealthily drawing the swords of the sleeping warriors from their sheaths, each woman stabbed the man lying at her side.

'The husbands and the lovers crouching outside the heavy ramparts heard the signal that had previously been arranged between them. They broke in over the unprotected ramparts upon the sodden, hated foe, and finished off the ghastly work their womenfolk had begun.

'And then it dawned upon me, the explanation of the whole grim affair. Was it not All Hallowe'en? A weird day to choose to walk alone on the haunted Chase. The dead had come back to life to live over again the fearful days of yore. We had fled, the dog and I, but even away from the camp some of the dead had stalked us.'

Beaminster

There are several strange ghost stories from Beaminster, most of them associated with the home of the town's famous Monmouth rebel, John Daniel. Sadly the town possesses few old houses. In 1644, during the civil war, Prince Rupert – a supporter of Charles I – billeted his soldiers in many of the houses; some were French and some were Cornish. Before long quarrels broke out and the two groups started fighting one another. Prince Rupert, finding himself in a hostile town with a divided army, withdrew his troops and burnt the town, causing great distress to the inhabitants for such goods as they managed to save from their burning houses were looted by the soldiers.

Seven years later, in 1651, Beaminster was described as a collection of blackened, ivy-covered ruins. Only East Street and part of Church

Street seemed to escape the fire. In 1684 the town was again burnt, this time by accident, and the same happened again in 1781. In 1685 many Beaminster men joined Monmouth, the 'Protestant Prince', and after the disastrous Battle of Sedgemoor, many of the men who survived became victims of the Bloody Assizes.

A well-authenticated and early ghost that apparently appeared in broad daylight concerns another 'John Daniel'. The story first appeared in an issue of *The Gentleman's Magazine* in 1774; a story that is recounted in the official guide to the church of St Mary.

In the eighteenth century a gallery of the parish church of St Mary served as a schoolroom and at lunch time on 27 June 1728 a dozen or so lads loitered in the churchyard, playing with a ball; four of the boys were in the 'school' when they were somewhat startled to hear a noise that sounded like something striking a brass pan. Thinking one of their friends was hiding and trying to frighten them, the boys spread out and searched the building but found no one.

As the boys were thinking they must have been mistaken they heard a second noise that seemed to orginate on the stairs leading up to the gallery: this time the sounds seemed to resemble part of a religious sermon and this was succeeded by sounds of a congregation singing. After these sounds had ceased one of the boys went into the schoolroom, looking for a school book, and there he saw, about six feet away from him, a coffin lying on one of the benches. He ran back to his friends, told them what he had seen, and together the five boys returned to the door of the schoolroom and there they all saw the apparition of John Daniel, whom all but one of the boys had known and who had been dead for more than seven weeks. He seemed to be sitting some distance from the coffin.

The first boy to recognise the ghost was John Daniel's half-brother and he immediately cried out: 'There sits our John with such a coat on as I have.' During the lifetime of the deceased boy the half-brother and he had usually been dressed alike. The ghost boy appeared to be holding a pen in his hand and there was what looked like a book beside him but his half-brother began to be frightened and thinking someone was playing a joke on him, he said, 'I'll throw a stone at him…' Some of the other boys tried to dissuade him but he picked up a small stone and threw it – whereupon the form of John Daniel, the pen, the book and the coffin immediately disappeared.

Understandably the incident created considerable interest in Beaminster and each of the boys concerned was examined and questioned individually by a magistrate, Colonel Brodrepp. All their stories agreed, even to such details as the size, shape and design of the hinges on the coffin lid; a description that tallied with the coffin in which John Daniel had been buried.

One of the witnesses, a boy of twelve, had recently joined the school and had not known John Daniel in his lifetime. This boy's story was particularly interesting in as much as his account was an exact description of the dead boy – and he added one item which the other witnesses had not apparently noticed. He said that a white cloth or bag was wound round one of the hands of the figure he had seen. It was subsequently established that the woman who had laid out John Daniel for burial swore on oath that she had taken such a white cloth from the boy's hand, it having been wound round his hand which he had injured a few days before his death.

The body of John Daniel had been found in a field, a short distance from his home, and the boy had been buried without an inquest being held after his mother had testified that he had suffered from fits. After the appearance of his ghost, the body was exhumed and it was established that the boy had in fact been strangled, although no steps appear to have been taken to bring to justice whoever may have been responsible.

Rodney Legg in his *Mysterious Dorset* (Dorset Publishing Company, 1987) recounts the tale of Amanda Allsop who revealed stories of a ghostly Lady in Blue who haunted Bridge House, the Tudor building at the corner of Whitcombe Street where the rebel John Daniel had once lived. In the early 1900s Bridge House had been owned and occupied by Mr and Mrs James and it seems to have been during their residence that the unidentified Lady in Blue made her initial appearance. She never seems to have frightened anyone and her occasional appearances soon became accepted as a matter of course. She was first seen by Evelyn Leigh, a friend of the Jameses who was staying at Bridge House. One morning she asked her hostess why she had been walking about the house so late the previous night and wearing high-heeled shoes. Soon various people claimed to see a tall, slim woman dressed in a long blue dress and wearing high-heeled shoes; she was most frequently seen in the hall and Mrs James in particular seemed to become quite accustomed to the mysterious figure. There are reports of the same lady having been seen, from time to time, for more than twenty years.

As reports of her appearance at Bridge House grew less frequent, the house next door was sold to an industrial concern, something the last owner of the property had been much against. Before long this property was demolished and two local historians took some twenty photographs for posterity. On two of the photographs there appears to be an indistinct shape which in each case can be interpreted as that of a tall woman in a long dress and wearing high-heeled shoes. Certainly no such person, according to the historians, was present at the time the photographs were taken. I have not personally seen these photographs so I cannot comment authoritatively.

Mrs Vera Bewbery of Ludwell, near Shaftesbury, told Rodney Legg of her experience at Bridge House in the 1930s, when she went there to nurse an elderly sick woman. She was allocated the so-called Guest Room which she found to be spacious and overlooking a stream and cottages; but she found great difficulty in getting to sleep each night. There was a restless, unnatural feeling about the room at night which eventually caused her to ask whether she could have a different room. She was found another, nearer to her patient, and a new housekeeper moved into the Guest Room.

After her first night in the room the housekeeper said she had been awakened by a distinct knock on her door in the middle of the night but on answering it had found no one there; she had then been unable to get back to sleep and couldn't help thinking there was something odd and queer about the room.

In 1939 the housekeeper was moved to a back bedroom to make way for the owner's nephew who had arrived from overseas to join the RAF and he moved into the Guest Room. Next morning this young man came down to breakfast, very tired and puzzled. He said he had woken up to find his bedclothes had been pulled off and he had fallen out of bed and knocked over a small table, smashing a bedside lamp and for the rest of the night he had tossed and turned with hardly any sleep.

Eventually Rodney Legg's informant learned the story associated with the haunted Guest Room from another servant. Apparently a murder had been committed in the room and blood had seeped through the ceiling of the room below, causing a stain that could never be removed. It seems a dirty cream-coloured patch marks the spot to this day.

Bettiscombe

Perhaps the best known story of haunting in the whole of Dorset is associated with Bettiscombe House. This lovely Queen Anne mansion, nestling in the shadow of peaceful Dorset hills, was called 'The House of the Screaming Skull' because of the yellowed skull preserved there and because of the strange manifestations that are said to have occurred when the skull was removed from Bettiscombe House.

The story was first related in print by J S Udal, a High Court Judge and collector of folklore who, in 1872, told of the human skull that had been at Bettiscombe for many years. He added that, according to tradition, if it were removed the property itself would rock to its foundations and the person responsible would be dead within a year.

One legend says that the skull is that of an African brought to England by Azariah Pinney – from whom a later owner Michael Pinney was descended – and who declared, just before he died, that he would never rest until his body was buried in his native land.

According to another story the skull is that of a black servant who was murdered; still another says that the skull was brought to England by Azariah Pinney and belonged to a faithful old black servant who died in his master's service abroad. Yet a fourth story suggests that the skull is that of a young woman who died at Bettiscombe – some say after a long illness, some say she was murdered. Near the place where the skull rested for many years, immediately under the roof, there is a priest's hiding place, which might have some connection with the mysterious skull.

Azariah Pinney was the son of the Reverend John Pinney who died in 1705 and he lies buried at Bettiscombe. Both Azariah and his brother John joined the ineffectual Monmouth rebellion and were found guilty of high treason by Judge Jeffreys in 1685. John was hanged and Azariah shipped to the West Indies as a slave. It may be that years later he brought back this memento of a trusty servant whom he had named 'Bettiscombe'. At all events it is said that soon after the servant was buried in the local churchyard, screams were heard, animals on the farm died, crops failed and the house seemed to rock, but after the body was exhumed and the skull taken into the house, all was quiet.

Among the stories associated with the skull one states that years ago a tenant farmer threw the skull into the duckpond opposite the house and a few days later spent hours raking the pond until he found the skull: for he had been much disturbed by noises of all kinds during its absence and was only too glad to have it back inside the house. Another tale tells of the skull being buried nine feet deep and working its way back to the surface. It is said to have been heard screaming at the turn of the century, screams that reverberated throughout the house and were heard by villagers and farm workers in addition to the occupants of Bettiscombe House. In 1914 the skull is said to have sweated blood.

In 1963 the skull was examined by a professor of Human and Comparative Anatomy at the Royal College of Surgeons who decided it was probably that of a female aged between 25 and 30, rather small but certainly European.

Some years ago my wife and I were shown the Bettiscombe skull in the company of Lord Gibson, at that time Chairman of the National Trust, by hospitable Michael Pinney and his wife. I believe Michael sold Bettiscombe House and I wonder what has become of the skull.

Bovington

The Tank Museum here has the ghost of a German officer seen gazing at the Tiger tank which he presumably commanded and in which he may well have died in World War II. The lowest windows in the walls of the building housing the museum are eight feet from the ground, yet through them the form of the unknown German officer has been seen – 'frequently', according to Anthony Hippisley Coxe.

The authorities and museum guards know all about the ghost and refer to him, somewhat irreverently as 'Herman the German'.

Nearby, Lawrence of Arabia's whitewashed cottage, Cloud's Hill, where he may have found some peace towards the end of his tortuous life, is haunted. He once told Lady Astor, 'Nothing would take me away from Cloud's Hill,' but five days later, on his way home from Bovington Camp, as he roared along the road on his beloved Brough Superior motorcycle, he had his fatal and still puzzling crash.

Stories of his ghostly form, seen entering Cloud's Hill in Arab dress, began to circulate shortly after his tragic death, and over the years there have been many visitors to this National Trust property who have had no knowledge of the ghost but have been bemused to see a figure they have taken to be an Arab disappearing into the tiny cottage ahead of them; yet there has been no sign of any such person when they have followed the white-robed and silent form inside.

What may be a psychic echo associated with Lawrence's accident is the throaty roar of a powerful motorcycle that a number of people have claimed to hear, rushing towards them, often just before dawn; sounds that cease abruptly when the invisible machine is seemingly a short distance away.

As I said in my book *This Haunted Isle* (Harrap, 1984), 'Perhaps that last journey that Lawrence took has somehow become impressed for ever upon the atmosphere and perhaps his love of the place has lived on and sometimes becomes crystallized into a visible form; at all events it seems indisputable that the moving spirit of the Arab revolt is seen from time to time, visiting again the little cottage that he loved, as he did so often during his lifetime – but in Arab costume? Perhaps that is how he most often thought of himself; who knows?

Incidentally, a few years ago a correspondent from St Leonard's-on-Sea, Mrs Peter Brown, was kind enough to send me an account of her experience of seeing what might have been the ghostly form of T E Lawrence – but not in Arab robes and not at Cloud's Hill:

'My husband and I were on holiday, touring in a motor-caravan, and on 17 May 1967 we visited Cloud's Hill for the first time; from there we went to Wareham, parking on the quayside facing the bridge which was on our right. Children, who had been playing by the water, had all gone home by six o'clock and all was quiet. Sitting in the cab my husband was checking the map and I took out my compact and was halfway through using the lipstick when I chanced to look up from the mirror. Any reasoning at what I saw was taken out of my hands... the shock seemed to stop my heart for a couple of beats and I felt as one must feel when drowning; if it had missed another beat my husband might never have known why I was not with him anymore!

'As I had looked up, TEL was standing there on the bridge. He was standing in the first niche of the bridge, his arms resting on the parapet, and he looked round slowly to meet my eyes and, as long as I returned his gaze, he never turned away. Did the experience last for seconds or for minutes? I do not know. When I lowered my eyes I stuttered to my husband something about who was there. He looked, but saw nothing, but he did not tell me that at the time. We drove away and I could not look up at the bridge; it was almost as though an iron hand held my head down.

'I was very puzzled for he had been dressed in RAF uniform and I think I had seen a photograph of him like that but I had assumed it to be Army uniform. Later Mr Les Perrin, who owns TEL's last Brough motorcycle, showed me an article about Lawrence and a photograph of him just as he had appeared to me, in RAF dress, a photograph taken in India.

'I recall that his face was very, very red; his eyes seemed to be screwed up against the light, although in fact the sun was behind him. Now I know one can see him like this in a photograph in Richard Aldington's *Lawrence of Arabia* (Collins 1955) and one taken, I think, at the same time in *The Letters of T E Lawrence* (Cape, 1938) captioned "Miranshar 1928"; but that I saw some form of Lawrence that day at Wareham I am overwhelmingly convinced. By the way, we have been to Cloud's Hill and Wareham every year since, even if only for a day, but I have never seen Lawrence, if it was Lawrence I saw, again.'

Brownsea, off Poole

The castle here, which is private property, has a ghost. I am informed of this by a correspondent who tells me that a friend of his worked there on the catering staff throughout one summer and she claimed to see a frightening apparition.

It seems that the young lady in question, Miss T Muster, stayed in a room which she shared with another girl who also worked in the castle. One night they sat talking until about 11.30 pm and then they went to bed. They were accommodated in an extension built at the back of the castle to house staff. The girls' room was on the ground floor and running alongside it was a walkway.

The two girls were just dropping off to sleep on this occasion when Miss Muster opened her eyes and saw a form bending over her bed, a form that she described as a 'large black figure'. Apparently it had wide shoulders and a hooded head but she could not see the face; the whole form was almost like a silhouette. As she lay trying to decide what she was looking at and what her best plan of action was, her companion called out: 'Stop tugging at my pillow…' In fact the two beds were well separated and there was no way Miss Muster could have reached her friend's pillow, but she was too absorbed by what she was seeing to take much notice at the time.

After a few moments Miss Muster realised that her companion had fallen asleep. The dark shape was still there and Miss Muster pulled the bedclothes over her head and eventually fell into a troubled sleep.

Some time later Miss Muster heard from one of the local islanders, who knew nothing of her experience at the time, that there was a story concerning a ghostly dark man wearing a cloak who was supposed to walk in the area of the walkway near her room. She also learned that another room in the castle was reputed to be haunted – a room that was sometimes used by guests – but she did not learn the nature of the reputed haunting.

Bryanston

Situated one mile west of Blandford, Bryanston nestles on the bank of the River Stour which runs through the formerly extensive parkland that stretched from Durweston in the north to Blandford in the south.

My good friends Peter and Hazel Whitworth ran the Post Office store there and they republished a 50-year-old brief *History of Bryanston*, as collected by the 'splendid ladies of the Women's Institute'. They were good enough to draw my attention to a couple of ghost stories included in it.

The Portman family purchased the Bryanston estate from the Berkeleys in 1685. In 1778 they built a large house close to the river, perhaps rather too close. At all events, after the death of Viscount Portman in 1888 a new house, later known as Bryanston School, was built on higher ground and a new church was erected from stones of the old house when the new property was completed.

'There are some interesting stories told of the former Bryanston House and, like many other old houses of its day, it had its ghost. A maid who lived there about 1870 said her bedroom door opened after she was in bed at night, and a lady walked in, came and stared at her, frightening her very much, and then went away. The maid asked the housekeeper at breakfast next morning who the lady was who had mistaken her room, and was told there were no visitors in the house.

'Later in the day the housekeeper showed her over the house and the maid suddenly pointed to a picture and said, "That is the lady who came into my room last night." The housekeeper answered in a very surprised voice, "Why, that is old Aunt Charlotte – she has been dead for years."

'An old nurse who was attending the Viscount Portman in his last illness said she often heard walking and talking in his Lordship's room at night. The first night she heard it, she went into the room twice and found Lord Portman asleep each time. In the morning she said to her patient, "I came in twice in the night thinking you had called, and I heard someone moving about in your room." Lord Portman did not seem at all surprised and replied, "Oh! that often happens, it is nothing to hurt."

'The ghost was supposed to have been seen wandering about after the house was pulled down, and an old woman said, "Ha! the Portmans will not have any luck now that they have taken the roof off a ghost."'

Hazel and Peter told me there has always been talk of a phantom pack of hounds hereabouts, 'the Portman Hunt', and there are many tales of one large hound in particular that seemed to have no head; indeed a retired schoolteacher, still living in the area, recalls seeing this headless hound when she was a girl.

Charmouth

During one of our annual visits to Bridport in the 1970s my wife and I made a point of calling at Charmouth Lodge, an old and attractive house in The Street, where we met Miss Joan Whittington – a direct descendant of London's most famous Lord Mayor – who told us of the ghosts that have been seen in the house and garden. She also showed us a copy of an old history of Charmouth which contained details of the White Lady of Charmouth Lodge, seen by the author's mother; of a ghost monk who walked there; and of such happenings as doors opening inexplicably and mysterious footfalls.

Miss Whittington told us she had herself seen the ghost monk. He wore a brown habit and she saw him, as distinctly as she saw us, in the garden. Interestingly enough the house has monastic associations but Miss Whittington never felt any fear when she caught sight of the apparition, rather a feeling of mild puzzlement, and she said she was convinced that he is a friendly ghost, possibly strolling where he and his brethren walked centuries ago.

The White Lady seems to be a less peaceful spectre. The story goes that she is the shade of a woman who was murdered in the house and whose body was dropped down a well, situated underneath the present dining room floor. The best authenticated sighting of the White Lady in recent years is probably the time she was seen by Miss Whittington's cousin, later the Reverend J Robinson, who was playing the piano in the dining room during a visit to Charmouth Lodge. Suddenly he became aware of the figure of a female dressed in white and she placed a cold hand across his face. 'I can still hear his scream,' Miss Whittington told us.

There are reports of the same figure being seen elsewhere inside the house, suddenly sweeping down the stairs wearing a full flowing skirt; and also in the garden where it was noticed she made no sound as she 'walked' across the flag stones. Conversely, the sound of her footsteps have been heard many times along a passageway inside Charmouth Lodge, when no form has been seen.

Christchurch

St Catherine's Hill, it is said, was originally planned as the site for the Augustinian Priory but, in common with similar stories elsewhere, ghostly activity prevented the fulfilment of these plans. No matter how many times building materials were taken to the top of the hill ready for work to commence, next morning they were found down at the foot of the hill and so eventually the monks had no option but to build their priory in the valley below.

From time to time I receive reports of ghostly monks or monk-like figures being glimpsed in the present priory gardens but if they are ghosts they are harmless shades walking where they used to walk in some way which we do not yet understand, momentarily visible and occasionally audible too. And yet are these monk-like figures always harmless? There have been several reports of such a figure standing at the top of the staircase leading to the tower, and some witnesses have said they have felt an unmistakable nudge as they have passed the form – not a pleasant experience at the top of a steep stairway.

There is a haunted chapel in the Priory Church. The little Draper Chapel, named after the last Prior of Christchurch, John Draper, who died in 1552, has, it would seem, been visited by this gentleman. His friendship with Thomas Cromwell is said to have persuaded Henry VIII to leave the church intact, although the monastic buildings were destroyed.

Some years ago a young lady remarked upon the 'man dressed like a monk' who had just passed her and disappeared into the Draper Chapel; a figure that had not been seen by anyone else at that particular time but other visitors on other occasions have reported seeing a silent, robed monk in the vicinity of the same chapel – a figure that disappears under mysterious circumstances.

A somewhat different psychic disturbance was reported in 1972 when congregations at the Priory Church were disturbed by seem-ingly inexplicable noises. One of the Norman arches was being restored at the time but the stonemason never seemed to be present when the curious tapping sounds were heard, for they were nearly always reported on Saturdays and Sundays when the restorers never did any work at the Priory. Other disturbances at this time included the mysterious opening of a door on the south side of the Priory and a strong and distinct smell of incense that was reported by, among others, the head verger, Ronald Smith.

Questioned about the strange sounds, the vicar, Canon Leslie Yorke, said at the time that he had not personally heard the strange sounds but certainly incense was never used in the Priory today and, he added, 'There have been many unaccountable noises in the Priory and I certainly trust the integrity of those who tell me they have heard the tapping sounds.'

According to Donald Weeks' *Corvo* (1971) the doctors' house in Bridge Street, where Frederick William Rolfe, 'Baron Corvo', lived for a time in 1889 and during 1891, is haunted by a soldier in Cromwellian uniform who appears in the garden together with his horse.

North of the Priory Church, beside a backwater of the River Avon, at a place called the Three Arches Bend – from the triple-arched bridge that carries the main London railway line – aural and visual manifestations recall a tragic happening on 4 June 1935.

The classic Rattenbury murder case has been the subject of books, plays, radio and television presentations. Alma Rattenbury was legally acquitted, but publicly condemned, of having any part in the murder of her elderly husband by her young lover George Stoner. The case was a sensation in its day and although Alma was never the dissolute woman portrayed by the press and by the prosecuting counsel, it was a broken woman who emerged from the Old Bailey trial after Stoner was found guilty and sentenced to death by hanging.

Four days later Alma Rattenbury went alone to the Three Arches Bend at Christchurch, stabbed herself six times, piercing her heart three times, and stumbled into the shallow water. Later Stoner's death sentence was commuted to life imprisonment; he served seven years, married and lived in the same house in Bournemouth where he had lived with his parents all those years ago.

At the spot where poor, depressed Alma took her own life there is still an air of quiet mystery, a curious expectancy, a terrible sadness on occasions that many people have noticed. It is particularly noticeable on still June evenings when a solitary, silent female figure has been seen sitting in the long grass where Alma sat, penning a last pathetic note before she stood up, walked to the water's edge, stabbed herself repeatedly and then fell face down into the quiet waters.

Corfe Castle

This picturesque and historic National Trust property has long had the reputation of being haunted. Here the eighteen-year-old King Edward (later proclaimed 'the Martyr') was murdered by the order of the preceding King's second wife Elfrida who wanted her son Ethelred – later known as the Unready – to be king.

Something of this ghastly deed and others in succeeding centuries seems to have lingered at this poignant spot and there are stories of a strange and unearthly light hovering about the place; of a mysterious ray of light sometimes being seen; of inexplicable flickering lights; and of dark and frightening figures, including a figure that resembles a headless woman drifting across the road below the castle.

Such a figure was seen by John Seagar, a local man, in 1967 and, according to newspaper reports, by three strangers in the area in 1976. Some researchers think the figure may be associated with the nearby Manor House which, according to legend, is linked to the castle by a secret passage. Others think it may be Lady Bankes, whose husband Sir John Bankes purchased the castle in 1635. She defended their home against Cromwell's troops and it is on the road leading to the main gateway that this vague and mysterious spectre has been seen.

Incidentally the ghostly funeral procession of the young King

Edward is supposed to appear occasionally on Gold Hill, Shaftesbury, led by two men in Tudor costume leading pack horses up the steep cobbles.

Corfe Mullen

A couple of miles west of Wimborne stands the tall, triple-chimneyed and haunted manor house, Corfe Lodge, which harbours a gentle shade known as 'the Lavender Lady'.

In the 1950s workers on the nearby Lavender Farm distilled the essence of lavender and other perfumes that were sold in miniature pots at Liberty's and Heal's in London. Some workers on the farm claimed to have seen the inoffensive Lavender Lady in those days and there are also stories of a phantom coach and a male figure resembling John Bull – but it is the Lavender Lady who is the best-documented ghost. Her story was published in the *Poole and Dorset Herald* in July 1969, in a letter from Mary Cliff whose mother was a resident maid at Corfe Lodge for many years.

One night Mary Cliff's mother was disturbed by the sound of footsteps and what sounded like a door opening. As she opened her eyes she became aware of a figure standing at the foot of her bed; a beautiful young woman with her hair in long plaits, one on each side of her head. After seeming to bend forwards over the bed, she smiled and then drifted away.

In the morning Mary Cliff's mother thought she must have been dreaming but a few days later she had exactly the same experience again. When it happened yet a third time she became very puzzled and asked to be put in another room. She then learned that the figure she described had been seen by others, residents in the house – family and servants – and by visitors; but no one had said anything to her for fear of frightening her.

Mary Cliff claimed in her letter that her uncle, Billy Heckford, who worked at Lavender Farm, saw the ghost several times, both inside and outside Corfe Lodge, and she ends her letter: 'I may be a sceptic over many things, but I know my mother's story was true. The Lavender Lady really did walk in the rooms of Corfe Lodge long ago… and I have often wondered whether later inhabitants have witnessed any strange happenings.'

Dorchester

The Antelope Hotel once housed the courtroom used for some of Judge Jeffreys's Bloody Assizes following the Duke of Monmouth's 1685 rebellion.

It was in a room at the back of this hotel, where a window overlooks the room said to have been used by Jeffreys as a courtroom, that Ghost Clubber Dorothy E Warren had a very strange experience.

On three successive nights Miss Warren, a member of the Society for Psychical Research and an amateur archaeologist, found herself awakened by light streaming into her room through her open bedroom door, although she was quite certain that she had most carefully closed the door before going to bed on each occasion.

After the third time Miss Warren mentioned the matter to a chambermaid but she could find nothing wrong with the door or the way in which it closed and she could offer no explanation – although Miss Warren noticed that the girl looked at her a little oddly.

The next night, in addition to the door opening, Miss Warren was awakened by the sound of footsteps which appeared to go backwards and forwards in the next room beyond the top of her bed. As she listened she also heard an occasional 'clink' as of metal against metal. Looking at her bedside clock she found the time was 2.30 am and still the pacing continued until in desperation Miss Warren called out: 'For goodness sake shut up!' Much to her surprise the sounds ceased instantly.

Next morning Miss Warren made a number of enquiries, during the course of which she discovered that the room next to hers, from which the mysterious noises seemed to originate, had in fact been unoccupied, and in any case the thickness of the wall between the rooms would have prevented any but the very loudest sound being heard in her room. Puzzled but still disturbed by sounds from the empty room at night, Miss Warren was given a different room for the rest of her stay and there she slept undisturbed.

Other ghostly activity in Dorchester includes the sound of a door closing and of footsteps climbing a stairway and then fading away, a phenomenon frequently experienced by an inhabitant of the Old Malthouse in High East Street. The footsteps always went up the stairs and never came down. This witness maintained that on occasions he heard footsteps approach him, pass him, and continue behind him and times without number he heard footsteps crossing the floor above his head but when he went up to see who was there, he invariably found no one…

The church of St Peter's was said to be the scene of a ghostly appearance on Christmas Day 1814, when two churchwardens were taking a break after decorating the church. As they rested they both became aware that someone was sitting between them and it was someone they recognised: their late rector, the Reverend Nathaniel Templeman, who had died the previous year.

The apparition seemed to look from one to the other of the startled churchwardens and then he shook his head as he had done so often in life when he was disappointed with something. The figure rose without a sound and slowly 'floated' up the aisle and then sank and disappeared from view.

The story was accepted by everyone who knew the churchwardens and by later church people, and it is included in some of the historical memories of Dorchester. There is some evidence that the ghostly form of Nathaniel Templeman has appeared since then in St Peter's Church and that it does in fact still appear from time to time.

Dick Sheppard tells me there is a supermarket in Dorchester where the ghostly form of the dreaded Judge Jeffreys is supposed to appear at night, after the premises are closed, in the vicinity of the meat counter. Other people claim to have seen the unmistakable face of the 'Hanging Judge' peering at them out of one of the windows along the nearby passageway.

East Lulworth

The wide sweep of Worbarrow Bay has a spectral army that has been reportedly seen here since 1678. Hutchins, in his *History of Dorset* (1774), says the ghostly forms were seen one evening in December marching from Flower's Barrow over Grange Hill, overlooking Worbarrow Bay, making a 'great noise and clashing of arms' and as a result preparations for defence were made.

The ghost army of Purbeck is said to reappear when the world is at war and there were persistent reports of the 'army' being seen and heard during both the great wars. Those who know from experience say that it is possible to 'uncomfortably feel an inexplicable presence' and also to hear the thud of horses' hooves and the tramping feet of men and even sometimes to glimpse indistinct forms on those December nights when no rabbits or dogs can be induced to walk that haunted path.

Worbarrow Bay itself has a ghost smuggler. At the far end of the long and lonely bay a solitary smuggler was surprised, it is said, long ago by a party of revenue men. Not too familiar with the immediate area, the smuggler, in his haste and in the blackness of the night, ran the wrong way and found himself trapped, with the customs men hard on his heels while in front of him he faced the sheer, unclimbable, 550 ft (170 m) rock at Cow Corner.

Desperately seeking to escape, the hunted man ran into the sea but there, at the water's edge, so the story goes, the defenceless smuggler was finally trapped and his tormentors stoned him to death, his last gasps and screams mingling with the never-ending sound of the sea itself. And these gasps and screams are said to have been heard again and again in the intervening two hundred years, especially at the waning of the moon, and sometimes, too, a dark figure is seen splashing wildly, waist-high in the sea before it disappears beneath the waves with a desperate, drowned scream.

Godlingston near Swanage

Some thirty-five years ago I called at the house from which this hamlet takes its name, the grey-stone, mullion-windowed Godlingston, and there I talked with Jean Bowerman.

Years before, she had been told that the ghost of an unidentified lady walked in the garden beside a mellow, age-old wall; but Jean Bowerman never saw the quiet lady there although she did once sense that a presence was looking in at a window and the feeling was so powerful that she never forgot it. She told me: 'Had I been a dog, my hackles would have stood on end... I was never so frightened in my life and I fled!'

Afterwards, entertaining a former occupant of Godlingston to tea one afternoon, she was amazed to hear this lady relate that on at least two occasions her husband had seen the ghostly lady through that particular window!

Later still the ghost seemed to move indoors and to frequent an upstairs landing – a familiar spot for ghostly activity – and Jean

Bowerman told me she knows with a certainty that brooks no argument when the mysterious presence is there. 'Not that I'm afraid,' she told me, 'Let's just say I prefer to hurry past that landing and not to look behind me...'

Longham, Bournemouth

An apparition, known as the Grey Lady of Longham, has been seen in the vicinity of Berrans Avenue on many occasions. Most witnesses agree that she appears to be wearing a grey cape and sometimes she wanders through the back gardens of the Avenue and makes her way along the banks of the Stour. Nobody knows who she was or why she walks but I have noticed that the reports occur most frequently around the month of February.

One correspondent tells me that both he and his wife saw the figure from one of their upstairs windows. When it disappeared from sight behind a shed and then reappeared in the next garden, having apparently walked through a garden fence, they hurriedly went out into the crisp February twilight but they could find no trace of the figure they had seen. Where they thought they had seen the 'Grey Lady' walking, the snow was crisp and even and undisturbed.

Another correspondent tells me that there used to be a lonely cottage on the brow of a hill here that was occupied by an elderly man who lived alone. The place was reputed to be haunted and lots of people claimed to have seen the figure of a lady with long black hair sitting in one of the rooms. The figure had no actuality and was only visible from outside the house.

Lyme Regis

The Angel Inn has been the scene of a series of reported incidents of a ghostly nature. In 1967 Mrs M Noble, a widow and the landlady at the time, told me that she had never felt frightened or had the impression of anything working against her.

She had not actually seen anything she could not explain, but she had often had the distinct feeling that she was not alone in the property when she knew full well that she was. With her son away at school she even found this feeling 'rather comforting'. She believed the ghost, if ghost there was, to be that of a former widowed landlady of the inn.

She felt a distinct sympathetic attitude and in spite of the many odd things that happened – inexplicable doors opening, objects moved, and sounds that are difficult to explain – she felt that the presence, whoever it was, had suffered personal unhappiness and now, in some strange way, sought to protect and comfort her, or his, successor.

In 1975 a resident who lived just across the road told me she believed the ghost was that of old Lizzie Lawton who loved her public house and, although she didn't die there, I was told that she could not stand the thought of someone else running The Angel. From what Elsie Clark told me, it must seem likely that the ghost was indeed that of Lizzie Lawton, a lovely but very old-fashioned lady, whose ghost has also been seen by Mrs Clark.

She informed me that one afternoon she was having a nap and when she opened her eyes she saw a little old lady standing at her bedside. There was no mistaking the figure. She looked rather like the elderly Queen Victoria. She always wound her hair into a bun and she loved jewellery. Wearing a spotless white apron she stood there looking down at Mrs Clark for several seconds and then she completely disappeared. It is interesting to report that a visitor, staying at The Angel, awoke one night to find an elderly woman bending over him, a figure he took at first to be Queen Victoria.

During her lifetime Lizzie Lawton tried desperately to carry on at The Angel; she was very reluctant to move, and her daughter helped her all she could but the two women just could not cope and in the end they left. Deeply distressed Lizzie is supposed to have said at the time, 'Nobody's going to do the same here as I've done.' It sounded almost like a curse and it was quite out of character for her to say anything like that. She had always seemed to be a very kind person but she was a strong character and after her death she may have wished to return to the public house she had loved.

It was put to me that, curse or not, there had been a dozen proprietors at The Angel since Lizzie Lawton left in 1927. Gordon Hosie is reported to have seen the ghost of Lizzie when he ran the inn and he died a few months later. He went over to visit Mrs Clark after seeing the ghost and he was very upset by the experience. A later landlord and landlady, Ted and Eileen Bignal, both said they were aware of the presence of the envious ghost. On one occasion a glass cheese dish 'exploded' for no apparent reason; another time a drinking glass 'flew off a shelf' and shattered to pieces on the floor at their feet. 'It didn't drop off,' I was told. 'It jumped off, a distance of about two feet; it was quite inexplicable.' Ted Bignal was usually sceptical but he too came to be very puzzled over some of the strange happenings that were experi-enced. When Ted Oakes was landlord both he and his son-in-law Joe Wain were reportedly 'frightened to death' by a strange coldness and a sensation of something invisible being near them; an experience of which even their dog seemed to be aware.

The young son of one landlady said he saw 'an old lady' come out of a cupboard in a bedroom and on another occasion his brother said a phantom bent over his bed with a sad expression on her face'.

Another allegedly haunted establishment at Lyme Regis is the Royal Lion Hotel, situated close to the site of a former place of execution. In 1973 various strange experiences were extensively reported: a shape 'like drifting mist' in the dining room; the sounds of footsteps in the same area; a cold and chilly sensation in various parts of the hotel; the sound of an invisible entity entering the dining room; the sound of an organ playing; and something 'like a damp mist that seems to go right through you – turning you to jelly…'

One of the rooms on the upper floor is said to be haunted by the sounds of 'pitiful moaning' and the inevitable 'unexplained foot-steps'. Such sounds have been reported by members of staff and by visitors, not infrequently by people who have had no knowledge that identical sounds have been reported by other people.

The historic Great House in Broad Street at Lyme, now known as Chatham House, is said to harbour or has harboured at least two ghosts. The house once had a very sinister reputation and during the Monmouth rising of 1685 the owner was an ardent supporter of James II, thereby incurring the abhorrence and distrust of the largely Monmouth supporters of Lyme, especially when he actively assist-ed the dreaded Judge Jeffreys in his keen and brutal routing out of Monmouth's adherents. Indeed it is said that two men of Lyme Regis who had been condemned as traitors had their heads exhibited on the spiked iron gates of the house.

A number of strange happenings were reported at the house at the time of the owner's death, including 'a mighty noise', a 'great light in the air' and the falling-in of a gable of the house.

The second ghost at the house is that of Judge Jeffreys himself and tradition has it that his sinister figure walks in robes, wig, black cap and 'brandishing a bloody bone' whenever the house stands empty.

In recent years the property has been used as offices and shops but stories of strange happenings continue to circulate. Heavy footsteps that are thought to be those of the 'Hanging Judge' have been heard on many occasions – once by the manager of the shop premises.

Pimperne

Here there is a ghostly disembodied hand seeking to be re-united with its body which lies buried well over a 100 miles away in London. The 'haunting' is said to originate in 1780 when a certain trumpet major in the Dragoons, a man named Blandford, who later occupied his time as a poacher, was involved in some illegal hunting of deer at Cranborne Chase.

Deer stealing there had been growing more frequent and a party of local gamekeepers banded together and set a trap for the poachers. Blandford was surrounded and during the ensuing fight several game-keepers were badly hurt and one subsequently died of his wounds.

Blandford had one of his hands completely severed. He still con-tinued fighting but he was eventually overcome, captured and com-mitted to Dorchester gaol, only escaping transportation because of his wounds. Eventually he was released and he moved to London where he set up as a shopkeeper and where, in due course, he died.

Meanwhile the hand had been buried in Pimperne churchyard and over the years there have been a number of reports of the hand being seen, apparently seeking to be re-united with its body from which it was cruelly separated. The ghost hand is reportedly seen in a ride known as Bussey Stool Walk where presumably the skirmish took place. Much of the original woodland has disappeared but a meeting place of several paths in the vicinity is known as Bloody Shard Gate and a field between this spot and Bussey Stool Farm is known as Bloody Field. Both names presumably preserve the memory of the bloody fight that resulted in a ghostly hand.

Poole

Poole, so full of history, must by all accounts be the most haunted town in Dorset. That is as it should be for this natural harbour prob-ably saw the arrival of Celtic people before the now ancient earth-works were built on the hilltops; the Romans certainly used the place as a port; the Danes landed here to commit slaughter and reckless damage; Canute landed in 1015; Queen Elizabeth I approved Poole as a county distinct from Dorset; Charles II was here in 1665 with the Duke of Monmouth; and Poole has in fact been prominent in the history of this country since before recorded history and through all the succeeding years.

Parts of Scaplens Court, the Town Museum (once a town house) go back to the fifteenth century and the premises are said to harbour the ghost of Agnes Beard. Agnes was a maid to Mistress Alice Greene and they were both murdered in the house in 1598. Research has revealed that William Greene was a wealthy merchant and when he died he left his widow £200, a large sum for those days.

Three local rascals, Richard Parmiter, Robert Hill and Gowin Spencer, heard of this 'fortune' and devised a plot to steal the money; a plot that involved the then mayor of Poole, John Beryman, who lived in the house adjoining Scaplens Court.

When they broke into the house the would-be robbers disturbed the maid Agnes Beard who was having her supper in the kitchen; they quietly silenced her by a blow to the head with a hatchet and leaving the dying girl they also silenced a dog that threatened them. They then went looking for the widow and her money.

They quickly found both. The widow was murdered by stabbing and the money was stolen but the perpetrators of this brutal crime were soon caught. A lengthy trial ensued and eventually Robert Hill was hanged in 1599. Thereafter, it is said, and still to this day, the ghost of the unfortunate Agnes Beard has haunted the rooms of Scaplens Court; but of the equally brutally murdered Alice Greene there have been no reported sightings.

Joan Patch is convinced the place is haunted. 'Some of the attendants,' she says, 'have seen a lady wearing an apron coming from the buttery across the courtyard and going upstairs.' There have also been reports of the sound of a dog barking that has no natural explanation, but Mrs Patch has always found the house to have 'a warm and pleasant atmosphere' although she has had experiences there. 'I have often felt there is somebody there although I have never seen Agnes – if the ghost girl is Agnes – but I have seen the ghost of an old man.'

In fact Mrs Patch has seen the ghostly form of a man with a white beard and wearing a cloak standing in a room three times over a period of two years. 'He's rather lonely,' she says, but not in the least frightening.'

Mrs Patch has very different feelings about the 400-year-old Byngley House in Market Street. There a curiously oppressive feeling has been repeatedly reported and has been known to cause people to come away feeling faint and almost as though they have been suffocated. These experiences are confined to one upstairs bedroom. Some years ago a gruesome relic was discovered at Byngley House: the remains of a mummified cat were found nailed to floor joists; prob-ably an attempt to ward off ghosts and evil spirits, but it does not appear to have been very successful.

The Guildhall Museum at Poole is said to house the ghost of an unhappy clerk who hanged himself in the building in the nineteenth century and unexplained footsteps have been heard coming from the upper floors on many occasions. Once, when attempts were made to record the sounds, the recording machine malfunctioned and could not be made to work while it was there. This was reported by Mr Graham Smith, the museum curator.

Occasionally, according to reports, the high box pews and brass lamps in Skinner Street United Reformed Church are seen again from time to time, over 100 years after they were removed; and the Crown Hotel, in Market Street, has had the reputation of being haunted ever since the landlord, Alan Brown, started to convert some outbuildings. The sound of a body being dragged along the floor has been reported; a vague fluorescent shape moves down a stairway and piano-playing emanates from a room that contains no piano.

In 1966, Mr D Browne, visiting England from Australia, decided to conduct some experiments in an effort to disprove the haunting, but Mr Browne encountered more than he bargained for and he later described the event as 'the most eerie I have ever had in my life'. Among other things he bolted the door of the loft in the old stables but, as he walked away, he saw the door slowly open.

Ghost Clubber Dr Peter Hilton-Rowe visited the Crown and was impressed by the evidence. Once when the piano-playing had been heard and immediate investigation carried out, tools and nails in the room fell onto the floor for no apparent reason. Dr Hilton-Rowe told me there was a story that a former landlord, many, many years ago, incarcerated and then disposed of his two deformed children in a hayloft that later became one of the outbuildings. In an attic here a hidden room was discovered in 1966, a room that had no door.

In 1975 a series of terrifying sounds, resembling children rushing about in panic and screaming, alarmed frightened neighbours and tradesmen – and one milkman refused to deliver milk to the back door after hearing them. Children, according to J P Chilcott-Monk, have seen the apparition of an old woman in the upstairs part of the present hotel, when there has been no human person there; and at one time most of the residents of the hotel were reportedly conscious of waves of chill air, almost like icy breaths, in certain parts of the hotel.

In 1977 the old courtyard is said to have resounded with the sounds of stamping horses' hooves and the creak and grind of horse-drawn vehicles, although at the time the courtyard was full of stationary cars.

Other reported ghosts in Poole include a poltergeist-like entity, nicknamed 'Jenkins' who caused considerable damage, disturbance and distress to the occupants of a shop at 71 High Street in 1964 and again twelve years later. The appearance of a smiling man, wearing old-fashioned evening dress, has been glimpsed on the stairs here. When reports of the disturbances were published in a newspaper, a reader from California revealed that she had lived in the house from 1950 to 1963 with her two daughters. 'We were all aware of "unseen" occupants,' she wrote, 'whom we called "Mr Jenkins". I saw him once. He was quite a young man dressed in a dance suit and wearing a high white collar… my father was staying with us at the time and although we had not mentioned "Mr Jenkins" to him, he told us one day that a very rude young man had passed him on the stairs, almost pushing him to one side.' Objects and furniture also used to move by themselves. Since the property has been replaced by a modern building there have been no further reports of disturbances.

Another shop in Poole High Street has, or had, a cigar-smoking ghost! He was never seen but the strong aroma of cigar-smoke was repeatedly noticed in the ladies' fashion shop. The staff came to call him 'Charlie' and he seemed to bring a happy atmosphere with him, the manageress at the time stating: 'We are always very happy when he comes; it's a nice day and there are always lots of people around.' It has been suggested that 'Charlie' may have been a smuggler who once knew the old three-storey building – and in the next door building the body of a woman was once found walled-up in a cupboard.

It has been noticed that structural alterations often seem to trigger psychic activity. This was seemingly the case in 1973 when a young building worker, Rick Burgess, found himself face to face with a ghost when he was engaged in converting two eighteenth-century houses into a fully modernised Georgian style residence, at the corner of New Street and Cinnamon Lane in Poole Old Town.

At 9.30 one April evening, when he was working in an attic room behind the centre dormer window of the property, he suddenly became aware of a movement out of the corner of his eye. 'The room was lit, so was the landing a few feet away, and the room opposite. I distinctly saw a man disappear from the landing and pass into the other room. There was no sound and I didn't see or hear him come upstairs. He seemed to disappear round the corner in one big stride. He was wearing a long coat; it could have been a frock coat of a tweedy green colour. He had his back to me as I looked and I noticed that he had long, dark hair and it could have been tied at the back.'

Rick and his mate, Ian Stewart, went into the room where the figure had disappeared, but no one was there. Later, Rick took his wife Dilys, 'who is more sensitive in these matters', to the house. She felt nothing in the room where Rick had seen the figure disappear but in a room downstairs she felt distinctly uneasy and said the atmosphere there had made her flesh creep.

A building on the quay at Poole that was once a mill and then a blacksmith's forge has been the scene of odd sounds and happenings over the years. The property was in all probability used by smugglers in days gone by and noises associated with that activity have repeatedly been reported, together with the sound of a door slamming which has no physical explanation. Stories of a tunnel running from the building to a spot close to St James's Church lend credence to tales of smuggling and contraband, activities that may have left behind a psychic echo.

And then there is the King Charles Inn, also in the Old Town. Here, in 1984, there were numerous reports of odd and apparently inexplicable happenings. It is a fact that psychic activity frequently interferes with electrical apparatus and at the King Charles the video game was 'interfered with' so often that the landlord, Brian Elderfield, decided in the end to get rid of the machine.

Unexplained footsteps have long been said to perambulate late at night in various parts of the inn, footsteps that have been heard by customers, staff and those in charge. Once, Brian's wife Cyn unmistakably felt 'something' brush against the back of her neck while she was in the lounge; their daughter Debbie heard, late at night, the voice of a young woman but it was not any of the family; Mrs Elderfield's wedding-dress and a pair of cuff-links are among those items that have disappeared without trace or explanation...

'We are convinced it is a ghost,' Mrs Elderfield said at the time. 'People may laugh at us but we know what we have experienced.' No ghostly presence was seen but the family's pet Alsatian refused to go into some of the rooms and on occasions became very agitated for no apparent reason. Research has suggested that previous landlords at the hostelry in Thames Street also experienced paranormal happenings.

Puddletown

A mile east stands ancient and haunted Athelhampton Hall where, according to James Wentworth Day, there are ghostly duellists; a monk wearing a black hood; the hammering of a cooper who once made wine barrels in the cellar; a lady in grey; and a phantom ape.

The last time I was at Athelhampton I was told the story of the phantom ape (which was in fact a tame monkey), dating from the fifteenth century – a story that stems from a pet that was inadvertently imprisoned in a secret passage where it died of starvation. There have been no reports of this animal ghost within living memory.

The lady in grey on the other hand is still seen from time to time, usually in the Tudor Room, sitting in a chair after the day's visitors have all gone. Once, mistaking her for a visitor, one of the guides announced in a loud voice that the house was closing and her party must have left; whereupon the lady in grey rose without a word and, without looking about her, walked silently towards the wood panelling lining the room and there disappeared.

The ghostly duellists, too, have been seen in recent years. A guest at the Hall was in the Great Chamber when she saw two young men come into the room and begin to duel with each other. She called to them to stop but she was totally ignored, and when she rang the bell no one answered. As she watched, helpless, she saw one man receive a severe cut on his left arm; the duellists at once ceased their fight and quietly left the room. Later the guest asked her host about the two young men whom she had not met but had seen having a more or less friendly duel. She was informed that there were in fact no young men staying at the Hall at that time and in any case she had already met all the guests.

While I was at Athelhampton I was told that the figure of a monk, wearing a black habit, had been seen within the previous few weeks, walking in the garden, but when he had been approached he had suddenly and completely disappeared. The sound of hammering, too, supposed to be the work of a phantom cooper, had been reported within the last year and although it was thought that there must be a perfectly logical explanation for the mysterious sound, no such explanation was found.

Sandford Orcas

The impressive Tudor manor house here has been the subject of considerable investigation and at one time some people thought it vied with famous Borley Rectory as 'the most haunted house in England'. However, most if not all of the ghosts that were said to haunt this enchanting house from 1965 to 1975 seem to have departed with the irresistible Colonel Francis Claridge who leased the house from the hereditary owner Sir Christopher Medlycott.

Earliest among the unexplained happenings reported by the Claridges was 'beautiful music', like a harpsichord or spinet, that seemed to hover in the air over the arched gatehouse; and this was followed by unexplained voices, footsteps and movement of furniture. Soon phantom forms joined the gamut of ghostly phenomena at Sandford Orcas: there was an old gipsy lady in a macintosh; a white horse; a man dressed in a long cloak and a black hat; a murdering priest; a sinister moor; six cowled monks; a girl in black; another man, from Georgian times, *seven* feet tall – who was attracted by young virgins; an old lady who sat in a chair; another old lady in a red dress; and the ghost of Edward Knoyle, a friend of Sir Walter Ralegh, was said to walk in the house he knew.

The list of phantoms and psychic activity seemed endless but Benson Herbert took a team of researchers to Sandford Orcas from his Paraphysical Laboratory and reported afterwards: 'a *prima facie* case has been made out for the house being haunted.' They believed they had verified five independent ghosts.

A party of Ghost Clubbers visited Sandford Orcas one summer day in 1973. It was not an investigative visit, as reported in some quarters, and was in fact just one of more than fifty allegedly haunted country houses that members visited over a fifteen-year period from the centenary of the Club in 1962 until 1977 when the prices of hiring coaches for such day visits became prohibitive.

Colonel Claridge and his wife entertained the party with some fantastic stories: the huge gargoyles on each gable laughed in the moonlight; there was the sound of rattling chains every night; there was a room in which it was impossible to take a photograph; there was a phantom that appeared regularly seven nights running each year; a room that screamed; a room where 'every night a man parades up and down, his footsteps heavy and clear…'; and so on and so on.

Unfortunately the ghosts multiplied to such an extent that credulity was stretched beyond breaking point; erroneous dates and 'facts' were paraded; dubious photographs were exhibited; publicity was welcomed and it seemed that the time was long overdue when the owner of the house was asked for his comments.

In 1979 Sir Christopher Medlycott told me, 'I don't believe the house is haunted; our family lived there for 44 years and never heard or saw anything.'

In 1988 a number of ghost sightings at the Mitre Inn were reported in a history of the village compiled by Sir Mervyn Medlycott.

Sherborne

The Old Castle stands on a hill above pleasure grounds where there is a stone seat, commonly known as 'Sir Walter Ralegh's seat' where, legend has it, the ghost of the courtier, soldier, explorer and author returns each Michaelmas Eve at midnight; some say he returns to his seat after sadly walking beneath the trees in the old grounds.

He came to Sherborne in 1592, as Lord of the Manor, the gift of a grateful Queen Elizabeth I. He tried to make the old castle habitable and comfortable and when he failed, he built a new house, the core of the present New Castle. There is no doubt that Ralegh loved Sherborne but he was eventually disgraced, his estates were taken from him by James I and he was beheaded in Old Palace Yard, Westminster in 1618 – which may be why he is reputed to return without his head.

There is a story that Ralegh, who is said to have introduced potatoes and tobacco into England, was sitting on his seat at Sherborne one day, quietly smoking a pipe when a friend saw him and, thinking he was on fire, threw a bucket of water over him!

Other ghosts at the Old Castle include a phantom child and apparitional horses. In his review of *Haunted Sherborne* (Abbey Press, Sherborne, 1975) Christopher Brown relates a story recounted to him by a correspondent whose father was a nightwatchman at the castle between the two world wars. He always said he never saw any ghost at the castle but he had heard ghostly sounds many times. He always maintained that 'often' before midnight there would be the sound of galloping horses gradually drawing nearer and nearer to him – and then the sounds would suddenly cease.

An early Ghost Club member, Lady Chatterton, daughter of the Reverend Lasalles Iremonger, prebendary of Winchester Cathedral, was the wife of Sir William Chatterton and in her *Memoirs* (1878) she records her well-remembered experience at the later Sherborne Castle:

'I could scarcely have been four years old when we were staying at Sherborne Castle, an old place belonging to Lord Digley. It was built by Sir Walter Ralegh and is situated on a height overlooking a large piece of water with the ruins of an older castle on the farther bank.

'The castle was so full on our arrival that my old Scotch nurse and I were put into a large room, which I afterwards heard was said to be the haunted room. Nobody would sleep in it, and strange noises were heard at night to come from it. My nurse did not know this at the time, nor did my mother.

'My impression is that I was much pleased to find myself in this large room, for it was on the third storey, and the views from its windows over the beautiful terrace garden, which sloped down to the water and the ruined castle beyond, enchanted me.

'I slept in a little cot which had been placed close to a large, old-fashioned bed of carved oak with red velvet curtains, where my nurse slept. In the middle of the night I was awoke by a brilliant light that shone upon the wall. As I looked wonderingly at it, figures of men fighting seemed to pass over it, like the reflections produced by a magic lantern. Groups of figures passed to and fro, shouting as they advanced and retreated. The colours were very vivid; I saw red coats and black, and flashing of firearms, and heard horrible noises.

'I was very much frightened, and looked round to my nurse for help. She was sitting up in bed, and to my still greater horror I saw she was not awake, but her eyes were fixed, though she seemed to be making signs to the figures, talking to them and motioning them to go away, while they were yelling and quarrelling.

'I could neither cry out nor move – I was so frightened; but continued to look at the strange appearance. Suddenly it vanished, and all was dark and silent. A feeling of horror and dread, which I still feel when I happen to think of it, kept me awake until the day dawned through the window curtains, when I went to sleep. I never mentioned this horrible scene to my nurse, nor to anybody else, till many years afterwards, when I told her about it, and asked if she had any recollection of it. She answered that she had not.

'We often stayed at Sherborne Castle afterwards, but I never heard of anyone being put into that room to sleep. It was directly over the one my mother generally had, and one night she was roused by a violent knocking overhead. She described it as of dead bodies falling or being thrown about on the floor overhead. My father heard it too, and as there was a little turret staircase that wound up to the floor above out of their room, he determined to go and see what it could be.

'He lighted a candle and ascended the narrow winding staircase. He found the door of this large and mysterious room open, but no one was in it. He had the courage (as I afterwards thought) to pass through the room and went out at the other door, which opened on the great staircase, and came down again to my mother. The strange noises had ceased, and they never heard them again.

'I often went into that haunted room when I was staying there afterwards. I used to stand near the large, carved oak bedstead, just where my little cot had been, and try to account for the strange effect I remembered so well. The vision or appearance had been on the wall opposite the windows, and I tried to fancy that the moonlight could have shone in and produced some kind of pattern on the wall. But the paper on it was a kind of dull green with a very slight pattern, and I remembered that the dark red damask curtains of the windows had been drawn, so that had the moon been shining no light could have come in, except through some small crevices, and this could not have formed the large vision all along the breadth of the wall, nor the lurid light that awoke me out of my sleep.'

Studland

One of Dorset's most original ghost stories must be the 'White Donkey of Studland' that is reputed to appear annually about five days before Christmas. The story is that a century or more ago an old man was riding a white donkey over the heath; possibly he was a smuggler for he carried brandy and had a fair amount of money on him.

A naval deserter is said to have learned of the old man's journeys and one night he lay in wait and murdered the old man and made off with the spirits and the money. The terrified donkey galloped off and was never seen again – except when it returns, a ghostly image still seeking its lost master.

Forty years after the event a Purbeck fisherman, Ben Pond, recalled the occasion when he was walking across the fringe of Studland Heath and he saw the phantom donkey. It was late, perhaps 11.30 pm, when he saw a white object about 100 yards ahead of him. It was a dark night but there was no wind. When he saw the object move, he thought at first it was a sheet of newspaper. Then it moved again and, deciding discretion to be the better part of valour, he began to make a detour round the object in his path.

Having warily made perhaps half the detour he intended, he looked again at the object he was passing and he then saw that it was in fact a white donkey!

Laughing at his previous fears he regained his pathway and looked back. There it stood, an innocent white donkey – but what on earth was it doing there, at that time of night? Suddenly, as he looked, it completely disappeared. One second it was there, as solid and real as anything, and the next second there was no sign of the conspicuous white animal in the blackness of the heath.

Next day Ben Pond's natural curiosity caused him to return to the spot where he had seen the donkey, fully expecting to find hoof marks in the soft peat and patches of sand. There was not a single hoof mark. Later he discovered that although there were more than forty donkeys in the area, not one of them was white; and, as time passed, he came across four other people who claimed they too had seen the ghostly white donkey of Studland, in each case a few days before Christmas. Ben Pond saw the donkey near midnight on 22 December.

Tarrant Gunville

Little remains of Eastbury, a once magnificent house built by Lord Melcombe, but it was an unlucky house and even the ruins were said to be haunted by the ghost of a suicide.

William Doggett was Lord Melcombe's steward at the time the extravagant building was being erected and when the steward found himself in financial difficulties he appropriated some of the building materials to raise funds for himself, hoping to pay everything back before he was found out. When Lord Melcombe suddenly announced his intention of visiting Tarrant Gunville to ensure that everything was going according to plan and that all was as it should be, the wretched steward went into the library and shot himself.

Where he expired, his blood is said to have left a stain that only disappeared when the house was demolished but even the disappearance of Eastbury could not eliminate the ghostly form of Doggett, which used to be seen in the park – some say the figure appeared to be headless – and usually near the still-standing park gates, wearing a wig and knee-breeches tied with yellow silk as was his wont in life. The ghostly form has most frequently been seen at midnight, the time, it is said, that Doggett shot himself.

During the demolition of the church where it lay, Doggett's body was found to be as fresh as the day it had been buried and on the legs were tied yellow silk ribbons: little wonder the local people used to think that Doggett may have been a vampire.

Uplyme

Situated on the county boundary just above Lyme Regis, Uplyme has several convincing ghost stories. In 1970 a nine-year-old boy left his friends and ran home saying he had seen a coach and horses that disappeared, but nobody believed him. He was less worried by what he had seen than by the fact that his friends questioned his truthfulness… and subsequent investigation proved interesting.

The place where the boy claimed to have seen the coach was on the old back way coaching road at Whitty Hill, at a point where there used to be white gates and where the road drops down to the hamlet of Rocombe.

The boy was riding his cousin's bicycle at the time and was some way ahead of his companions; at a point in fact where he was out of their sight. Suddenly he saw '…a big coach, a stage coach, like you see in pictures… the top part was red and the lower part black with gold trimmings. It had four horses, three were black and one was white; and the coachman wore a mask over his face, not covering it but over the top part, like an eye-mask; and he had a big red feather in his hat. There were two men riding outside the coach on top at the back. The coach came out of a white gate and headed towards me.

'I looked straight at it. Then I looked away for some reason, I can't remember why, and when I looked back again the whole thing had vanished! There wasn't a sign of it or where it had been. There was no sound but I thought the men had cruel faces and I wondered if they had a prisoner inside…'

It might be thought that the details the boy noticed were such as would not have been imagined or invented on the spur of the moment. Years later the boy, then grown up, still persisted in his story and related again all the details he had noticed. It is interesting that many such coaches, as the boy described, must have used that road in years past; and the manner in which the boy saw the apparition and the manner in which it disappeared have the ring of truth.

Not far away, the road from Uplyme to Yawl is reputed to be haunted by the ghost of the Duke of Monmouth. He landed at Lyme Regis on 11 June 1685 and must have ridden up this road in the early days of his rebellion. He was a popular figure and his ghost may be the subject of folk-memory but there are convincing reports of his form being seen here riding on a white horse, always at night and usually around midnight. He trots along at a leisurely pace and some say he rides at the head of a procession of his followers. There is a theory that such apparitions are seen and heard for years before they begin to fade and run down, almost like a battery, and then the visual part of the spectacle fades first, leaving the sounds before they too disappear as the centuries pass. It is an interesting fact that in recent years it has been more common for the sounds of this ghostly procession to be heard rather than anything being seen. Still other witnesses have simply sensed a mysterious 'something' in this area.

The rectory at Uplyme was haunted at one time. In 1873 the Reverend Brooke de Malpas Egerton had the living and he claimed to frequently see an old lady sitting in an armchair by the fire.

He decided that he must be suffering from hallucinations and one day he deliberately sat down on the chair that was at the time seemingly occupied by the apparition – which immediately disappeared! Next day, however, he met the same figure in a passageway of the house and he also encountered her in other parts of the rectory. He decided to contact the sisters of the previous incumbent and they immediately recognised his description of the form he had seen.

'Oh! that must be mother,' they cried. 'When we were there she was constantly appearing but we hoped that when we left she might have found rest at last.'

Weymouth

Some years ago a Ghost Club member sent in a firsthand account of what was undoubtedly a very strange experience: a ghostly old lady who had been seen on the seafront. I present the story in the exact words of Hector D Campbell:

'I was walking with my fiancée, Kathleen, on the crowded esplanade. It was a very hot day, yet as I passed one of the seats an icy feeling came over me and I noticed a strange smell. It seemed to be compounded of sulphur and decomposition. I felt impelled to look at the crowded seat, and my eyes caught those of an old woman who was seated in the corner. The glance which she gave me was diabolical in its utter malignancy.

'"Come on Hector, what on earth are you stopping for?" exclaimed Kathleen. Her voice broke the spell. I recovered my composure and we walked to the end of the esplanade. "Shall we go home by the road?" I suggested. "Oh no, Hector, it is longer, and hotter. Let's go back the way we came and perhaps we may find a vacant seat. If so, I will be glad to rest for a while." So we retraced our steps.

'Again the same icy coldness, again the same overpowering smell; yes, and again the same awful old woman in the same corner. Suddenly Kathleen stopped just opposite to her. "Why here is a vacant seat," she cried. "I will sit down for a moment." But I seized her and held her fast. "No, no, there is no seat there," I exclaimed. "Let me go at once; you seem to have gone completely mad, and blind, too, if you can't see this empty seat in the corner." She angrily threw off my hands; the old lady held out her arms invitingly to her and Kathleen sank into them with a sigh of relief.

'I must have fainted then, for the next thing I knew was finding myself flat on the ground with a policeman bending over me. "There now, sir," he said kindly. "You'll soon be all right. It was the shock that upset you, the doctor said." The shock! Had he seen the old woman too? "What shock?" I faltered. "Why the death of the young lady that was with you. She just sank into a seat and went off at once, of heart failure, the doctor said." It was heart-breaking, but as I gazed at her face I felt that the malignant spirit had been defeated, for I never saw a more heavenly smile than that on the face of my dear, dead Kathleen.'

I remember that I was especially interested to receive this report as I had already two independent reports of a ghostly old woman who sat at the corner of a seat here and who disappeared under inexplic-able circumstances.

The seventeenth-century Boot Inn, opposite the Old Town Hall, has long been reputedly haunted and when John Radcliff and his wife took over the hostelry in 1973 they were told that their predecessors said the place was very haunted. There used to be reports of the sound of sea shanties being sung at night – sounds that came from empty rooms; more recently there have been reports of the heavy tramp of boots from a ground floor room and the occasional glimpse of the figure of a dark seaman wearing heavy sea boots who is there one moment and gone the next... in this comfortable and popular inn.

Wimborne

According to Rodney Legg, *Mysterious Dorset* (1987), King's House in West Borough is haunted by a ghost who manifests each morning at six o'clock when a heavy door in the wall of an upstairs room is heard to open. The doorway is now blocked but, it seems, the sounds persist. Next door, Dickens House has a ghostly clergyman who appears out of a wall, opposite the blocked doorway in King's House so there would seem to be some connection between these two hauntings. The clergyman, according to a lady who stayed at Dickens House during the last war, was often seen, dressed in black and carrying a Bible under his arm; he is thought to be the Reverend Percy Newall who owned King's House, or Garden House as it was then called, for some 30 years more than a century ago.

A friend of mine lived at Onslow House when she was a girl and one day when she and her twin sisters were enjoying a summer party, she was going upstairs with one of her sisters when she noticed a little boy on the stairs. She said to him, 'You'd better hurry along, everyone else is outside.' He didn't reply or seem aware of her or of her having spoken. As she passed on up the stairs, her sister, just behind her, said, 'Who on earth were you talking to?' 'Why, that little boy,' my friend replied, turning round to indicate the boy – but she was just in time to see the back of him before he disappeared in the direction of the garden; her sister saw nothing.

Years later, after the place became a home for elderly people, my friend called at her old home and one of the residents said, apropos of nothing in particular: 'You know, it's funny, but there's always a little boy in Edwardian costume about the house; nearly all the old people here have seen him.'

Other reported ghosts at Wimborne include a monk-like figure seen walking by the Minster, although the Minster was never really a monastery, rather a college of secular canons. The Griffin Hotel has a room that is haunted, mostly at Christmas time, by heart-rending and echoing sobs thought to be those of a devoted daughter whose father died in the room. The ghost of a woman has also been seen in the same hotel many times; she wears a brown skirt and old-fashioned lace-up shoes and she has grey hair, but whether she is connected with the sobbing sounds is unknown. During the last war the ghost was frequently glimpsed trotting along between Bedroom Number Four and the bathroom, then suddenly she would disappear.

Nearby Badbury Rings are reputedly haunted by some kind of prehistoric 'Peeping Tom' and there have been many reports over the years of couples finding themselves being watched and then making the surprising discovery that the watcher is a diminutive, bearded and hairy man whose voice, leaping gait and general appearance put those who have encountered the figure in mind of prehistoric man.

There is a curious atmosphere here after dark, an expectant feeling that is difficult to explain. Such a figure was reportedly seen in 1977 when the description referred to 'a leathery, twisted face, distorted by terrible wounds' and it is thought the form may be that of an old warrior who died on this bloody battlefield.

Winterborne Kingston

During the course of a Ghost Club visit to the New Forest in 1987, Richard Sheppard, a former Manager to Bournemouth Town Council, told me about a story he had heard firsthand from an elderly correspondent, with whom he subsequently met and talked. Richard Sheppard has allowed me to use the gist of this fascinating experience which is in fact a paraphrase of the original document, a copy of which is in my possession.

It was September, 1935, and our informant, then fifteen years old, worked as a farm boy at Tomson Farm, near Winterborne Kingston. He was at the time known as 'the village boy' and twice a week at night when all his work was done he had to ride his bicycle to Winterborne Kingston and there go round to all the old folk, collecting their doctors' prescriptions and such like; then he would ride to Bere Regis, collect all the medicine, tablets and whatever else was required and return and deliver them at Winterborne Kingston.

This particular night he had a message to deliver to a farm much further afield; it was quite a distance for a lad of fifteen after a hard day's work, perhaps one-and-a-half or two hours journey, but the message was to the effect that a very old person was dying in the village and he had relatives to whom it was necessary to get an urgent summons. By the time he had delivered the message it was probably eleven or eleven thirty at night but it was a beautiful night, with a full harvest moon, the sky brilliant with stars, and it was still very hot and tranquil.

Feeling more than a little tired the conscientious lad cycled slowly back towards Winterborne Kingston. He had heard that there was once an old manor house somewhere in the woods around there and as he cycled past what could have been the drive to the manor house he thought he heard faint music. He got off his bicycle, leaned it against a tree and walked quietly in the direction from which the music seemed to come. He found himself on a well-kept lawn with a fountain in the centre; he stopped and looked at the water sparkling in the bright moonlight. Then beside the fountain he saw a young lad dressed in very expensive clothes, with shining buttons and jewelled shoes and he was wearing or carried at his side a jewelled sword. The music that had attracted our lad's attention was explained by the fact that the boy was playing a violin.

As the tired village boy listened he noticed that the boy was wearing a large hat with big feathers attached to it. There was something strange about the figure and its surroundings and our informant realised that he was sweating, but he was too interested to move away. He crept into the shadows of the trees and stood still, watching; suddenly the young gentleman stopped playing and looked straight at the puzzled lad. For a few seconds they just stared at each other, then the magnificently attired young man put his violin down, took off his big hat and gave an exaggerated bow; he then replaced his hat and started to play again.

Our village lad had no hat but he did the best he could by way of reply and he bowed and saluted. The manor house itself was ablaze with light and the startled lad discovered that he could quite clearly see into the house. He found himself looking into a big room, alive with people dressed in expensive clothes: ladies wearing dresses or gowns that reached to the floor and sparkling with lots of jewellery; gentlemen wearing long coats that reached to their ankles, and each one was carrying a sword. The men's breeches seemed to be tied just below the kneecap and they wore long stockings and shoes with either gold or silver buckles. Some of the people were dancing and some were drinking. In one far corner of the room there was a group of musicians, several violin players and someone was playing a harp. Footmen were walking around with silver trays loaded with expensive glasses and drinks: the footmen were dressed in long red coats buttoned down the middle and they were wearing wigs.

To the 'village boy' it seemed they must be a very rich company of people. Then the watcher noticed in particular two well-dressed gentlemen standing just inside the room by one of the bay windows, the moon shining full on their faces. They seemed to be having a heated argument. One of them threw the contents of his glass into the face of the other who immediately took off a glove and slapped it across the face of his companion. At the same time the music and dancing stopped and everyone turned and looked towards the two gentlemen. Feeling certain that something violent was about to happen, our watcher moved further back into the shadows, not afraid exactly but rather transfixed by the amazing sight. He was beginning to be aware that in some mysterious way he was in a different period of time.

The gentleman who had received the insult, who looked to be about twenty years of age, came running out of the manor, obviously in a vile temper; he made towards the fountain and then seemed to change his mind, turned, and ran back inside. There he tore off his coat, drew his sword and tested the blade. Now the other gentleman came out of the house accompanied by a very old man who was tall and thin and wore a black coat reaching to his ankles. He also wore a tall black hat and carried a long walking stick, the jewelled top glittering in the moonlight.

Other ladies and gentlemen then came out onto the lawn and formed a half-circle, some of the ladies holding handkerchiefs to their eyes as if they were crying or expecting to cry. The two young men now came out of the house, took up positions facing each other, briskly saluted with their swords and when the old man dropped a large white handkerchief, they set to with a will. Both seemed to be expert swordsmen and they thrust, parried and struck. Their swift actions soon showed the accuracy of their aims and ominous dark patches began to appeared on and about the clothing of each man. The fight seemed to continue for about ten minutes and then the one who had come out of the manor first seemed to get the upper hand; he made what should have been the final thrust but he slipped and like a flash the other drove his sword into the shoulder of his opponent and the fight was over.

Two of the ladies rushed to the wounded man; everyone seemed to be in a very distressed state and the injured man was hurriedly carried into the manor. By this time it must have been well past midnight and the shadows from the trees and the manor itself were getting longer and darker; it was also getting distinctly chilly and the moon was beginning to fade. Our village lad had moved further back into the shadows when he heard the sound of horses and wheels approaching. The wounded man now appeared at the door of the manor, there was a heavy bandage over and around one arm and he was helped into a coach. Two ladies and the elderly man with the stick also got into the coach which then tore away from the manor along the drive and disappeared at breakneck speed.

The watcher now saw the lights of the manor house being extinguished; but he could still just make out the outlines of other coaches and horses, perhaps six in all, pulling up. The carriage doors were opened and then closed. The party was at an end and everyone seemed to be leaving as quietly and as quickly as possible. Then something happened: a mist was coming out of the ground and pouring out from the trees and bushes, enveloping everything in its path. The frightened lad decided to leave! He found that he could just disting-uish the outline of the last coach and horses galloping out of the drive and he was about to follow when he realised that he had left it too late; there was now a strange and uncanny silence about the whole place, the mist had become thick and clammy so that he could hardly see a foot in front of him and he began to panic.

He ran wildly into the bushes, falling over some logs and stones and into a bed of stinging nettles; he tore his way through thick brambles, shouting now for all he was worth until he became hoarse… he ran around in circles, the mist getting thicker and everywhere becoming darker. His heart was beating and pounding like a bass drum. The mist closed in and he had almost given up trying to find the road out when he heard the sound of the early milk lorry on its way to Blandford. It gave him fresh hope and strength and he tore his way through the remaining undergrowth and through the fog towards the sound. As it grew louder he hurried faster until at last he found an opening and reached the open road just as the lorry came lumbering along. The driver saw the terrified boy whom he knew by sight; he stopped and when he saw the state of the lad's clothes and his arms and legs torn by the brambles, he asked what on earth had happened and why was the boy out there at that time of night?

Together they found the boy's bicycle and put it on the back of the lorry and set off for Tomson Farm. On the way the frightened lad told the lorry driver that he had ridden into the ditch and fallen off and knocked himself unconscious.

Back at the farm – where he had a good telling-off! – the farm people were about to send out a search party for him. The lad never mentioned the experience to anyone; he knew they would never have believed him. Two weeks later, on a Saturday, he rode out there again.

He found what was left of the manor house but there was a tree growing through the middle of the roof, or where the roof should have been; there were great gaping holes where the windows had been; the front porch had collapsed; the drive was just a cart track; where there had been a lawn it was overgrown with gorse bushes and stinging nettles; and the fountain had completely disappeared. The lad never discovered any explanation but over the years he did occasionally come across people who complained of curious experiences in the vicinity of that old, deserted and crumbling manor house.

In eighty years he never forgot a single detail of that night.

Wool

Jacobean Woolbridge Manor was once the seat of the Turberville family and the story of the phantom coach that is said to have been seen leaving the mellow manor house on gloomy autumnal evenings was used by Thomas Hardy in his *Tess of the D'Urbervilles*. The ghostly four-in-hand is supposed to travel from the manor to the site of the vanished Turberville mansion at Bere Regis, four miles away, but perhaps the reason that reliable reports of this arresting spectral coach are sparse is because the coach can only be seen, it is said, by those with Turberville blood in their veins. There is a story that some sixty years ago a local bus driver saw the coach-and-horses as he was crossing the medieval bridge near the mansion and stopped his bus to let the coach pass … perhaps he had a few spots of Turberville blood in his veins for none of his passengers saw anything.

Dick Sheppard tells me his understanding of the story is that the coach, which makes no sound, bears down upon the unsuspecting with frightening speed on nights of the full moon only but especially if such is Hallowe'en.

Wooth, near Netherbury

Daniel Dunglas Home is probably the most famous medium of all time. He was never caught cheating in many years of mediumship in many parts of the world and he was never exposed; in fact there is no valid explanation of his methods and seeming miracles. It is necessary to read Jean Burton's biography, *Heyday of a Wizard* (Harrap, 1948), to appreciate the whole remarkable story.

During his colourful life D D Home was often in some trouble or other, and one legal case and the attendant adverse criticism and publicity almost overwhelmed him. This was the celebrated Lyon versus Home case and concerned a certain Mrs Jane Lyon who possessed the not inconsiderable sum of £145,000 which she had inherited from her father; she had married Charles Lyon Esquire of Wooth Grange, as it was then called. Her husband, according to Mrs Lyon, was connected to the ninth Earl of Strathmore and they spent their honeymoon at haunted Glamis Castle. Being psychic she had attempted to contact her husband after his death and then one day she had met DDHome.

Soon there was talk of the 75-year-old childless widow adopting the 34-year-old medium and of her 'making him independent of the world' by providing him with £24,000. He took her name by deed poll and became Daniel Home Lyon when Mrs Lyon tossed in a further £6000. All this, Mrs Lyon later swore, was in response to messages from her late husband relayed through Home. In the end it was not proved that Home used undue influence, but neither had he been able to prove that he had not, so the verdict went against Home. Mrs Lyon, however, was ordered to pay Home's costs of the ten-day hearing as well as her own.

So Wooth Manor, as it has long been known, has seen some colourful characters and a number of mysterious happenings; the origins of some of them lost in the mists of time. For ten years my wife and I spent an annual holiday in a cottage belonging to Wooth Manor and we came to know the owner and his wife. On more than one occasion we visited the manor and heard all about the ghosts that were said to have been seen there. In one bedroom there was a very strange feeling and each one of us present at the time thought we sensed some invisible presence; it was quite overwhelming and something I have not encountered as strongly anywhere else. Another room was said to be haunted by a restless ghost searching for something – a form that had, we were told, been sensed and seen on different occasions by different people who had no previous knowledge of the reputed haunting.

One person who has sensed several presences at Wooth Manor is Amanda Allsop, daughter of the late Kenneth Allsop whom I had the pleasure of knowing. After her visit to Wooth she said it had been one of the strangest experiences of her whole life. When she arrived she knew nothing about any ghosts at Wooth Manor and her hostess asked her to visit four rooms in particular and see whether she could 'feel' any presence.

It was a beautiful summer day and the balmy and perfect weather in the garden contrasted strongly with the atmosphere Amanda found as soon as she went into the house; immediately she felt there was something uncanny, something strange and something she did not like inside the old house.

In the first room she was taken to, situated in the middle of the house, she felt a vague something but nothing of great moment; the second room she visited was light and sunny but she knew instinctively that some invisible presence was also in the room: someone or some thing she felt had come into it with them and was standing somewhere unseen – she could not tell whether it had once been human or animal, attractive or grotesque, but that something alien was in the room she was quite convinced.

In the third room she felt the presence – whatever it was – had preceded them and was already there when they passed over the threshold. Amanda experienced some slight embarrassment in trying to explain that there seemed to be some psychic presence in the room but otherwise she was not at all worried and she did not feel anything unpleasant was associated with the unseen occupant.

Finally, in the fourth room into which she was shown, Amanda felt the atmosphere and her own emotions change dramatically. Here again the room appeared to be light and airy, with no dark corners, yet the young visitor experienced a sudden and inexplicable feeling of urgency and anxiety. She felt certain there was some presence in the room and this time she felt she could go some way towards identifying it. She felt an overwhelming desire to find something – what she did not know. She looked under the bed, behind the curtains, inside furniture, all over the floor... eventually she gave up.

Although she still felt there was something to be found in the room, she knew she couldn't find it. When she gave up and explained her feelings and her behaviour to her hostess, only then did she learn the ghost story associated with the house and in particular with that one room, as my wife and I heard it more than once.

The ghost was said to be that of a lady dressed in grey who wore her hair in a bun. She has been seen in several rooms in the house but most frequently in the last room visited by Amanda Allsop. She is thought to have been a servant who, many years before, had been dismissed for thieving and she returned to look for the objects she had been accused of stealing and so prove her innocence. Some people who have seen the figure, however, said she was too well-dressed to be a servant and they thought she may have been a daughter of the house who had lost something she treasured, perhaps a ring or a piece of jewellery with sentimental associations.